This Journal Belongs to:

_____

_____

_____

Cough Syrup

½ oz dry Red clover flowers
or (1 cup fresh)
1 cup hot water
2 cup sugar

Boil, Reduce heat 10-15 minutes
STRAIN, place in glass jar
with a tight Lid - store in
frig or cool dark place.
Take 1 tsp as needed (lasts up
to year)

* can help ward off coming cold

* can dry and charge in moon
energy for good luck charm

Raccoon - keep away evil

Let my heart be broken with the things
that break the heart of God.

~ ROBERT W. PIERCE

How sweet the words of truth breathed from the lips of love.

~ J. BEATTIE

Cast your cares on the LORD

and he will sustain you;

he will never let the righteous fall.

~ PSALM 55:22

Our affections are our life.

We live by them; they supply our warmth.

~ WILLIAM ELLERY CHANNING

Those who run from God in the morning
will scarcely find Him the rest of the day.

~ JOHN BUNYAN

It is only with the heart that one can see rightly;

what is essential is invisible to the eye.

~ ANTOINE DE SAINT-EXUPERY

We find rest in those we love, and we provide

a resting place in ourselves for those who love us.

~ BERNARD OF CLAIRVAUX

_____

_____

_____

_____

_____

_____

_____

_____

_____

_____

_____

_____

_____

_____

_____

_____

_____

_____

I seek you with all my heart;

do not let me stray from your commands.

~ PSALM 119:10

Have a heart that never hardens,
and a temper that never tires,
and a touch that never hurts.

~ CHARLES DICKENS

Far away there in the sunshine are my highest aspirations.
I may not reach them, but I can look up and see their beauty,
believe in them, and try to follow where they lead.

~ LOUISA MAY ALCOTT

You may trust the Lord too little,
but you can never trust Him too much.

No one grows old by living —
only by losing interest in living

~ MARIE BENTON RAY

Nothing is impossible to the willing heart.

~ THOMAS HEYWOOD

How great is the love the father has lavished on us,
that we should be called children of God!
And that is what we are!

~ 1 John 3:1

Great thoughts come from the heart.

~ MARQUIS DE VAUVENARGUES

Nothing is sweeter than love, nothing stronger,
nothing higher, nothing wider, nothing more pleasant,
nothing fuller or better in heaven or on earth.

~ THOMAS À KEMPIS

Be not afraid in misfortune. When God causes a tree to be hewn down,
He takes care that His birds can nestle on another.

The best and most beautiful things in the world
cannot be seen or even touched.
They must be felt with the heart.

~ HELEN KELLER

_____

_____

_____

_____

_____

_____

_____

_____

_____

_____

_____

_____

_____

_____

_____

_____

_____

_____

We cannot fathom the mystery of a single flower,

nor is it intended we should.

~ JOHN RUSKIN

Above all else, guard your heart,

for it is the wellspring of life.

~ PROVERBS 4:23

Life begins each morning…
Each morning is the open door to a new world —
new vistas, new aims, new tryings.

~ LEIGH HODGES

_____

_____

_____

_____

_____

_____

_____

_____

_____

_____

_____

_____

_____

_____

_____

_____

_____

The way to love anything is to realize that it might be lost.

~ G. K. CHESTERTON

Have courage for the great sorrows of life and patience
for the small ones; and when you have
laboriously accomplished your daily task,
go to sleep in peace. God is awake.

~ VICTOR HUGO

The heart has no secret which our conduct does not reveal.

We do not know what to do with this short life,

yet we want another which will be eternal.

~ ANATOLE FRANCE

Delight yourself in the Lord
and he will give you the desires of your heart.

~ PSALM 37:4

_____

_____

_____

_____

_____

_____

_____

_____

_____

_____

_____

_____

_____

_____

_____

_____

_____

_____

Living means making your life a memorable experience.

God not only hears our words,

He listens to our hearts.

Where your pleasure is, there is your treasure.
Where your treasure is, there is your heart.
Where your heart is, there is your happiness.

~ AUGUSTINE

Let love and faithfulness never leave you;
bind them around your neck,
write them on the tablet of your heart.

~ PROVERBS 3:3

Any time that is not spent on love is wasted.

~ GOETHE